J. Jones

Life in Motion

Gathered in Poetry

ISBN: 978-0-9996132-3-8 e-book

     978-0-9996132-4-5 paperback

WriterLostInWords.wordpress.com

For family, you know the one you create throughout your life because they will always be the ones supporting you through every crazy adventure you embark upon.

Table of Contents

Laugh with Me
A Pen and Words
In Seconds We Drown
Protestor
Let Me
Enough
Aging
To Be Held
On Espiritu Santo
Walk with Me
A Walk in the Forest
Eve is My Hero
Don't Shoot
Time
Who Spilled the Glitter?
The Return
I Failed
Just Another Dinner
Gone
555 Lost
Lessons Learned
A $2 Dream
Two Not Four
Reality
Deeds
Today
Life's Clutter
Sailor Ashore
Humanity
Draped in the Country's Flag
Find Yourself
The Door Unlocked
The Past
Educators
Work
How
Again
Missing
John Doe
Born Free, Die Free
Sounds of Summer
Teacher, My Teacher

To Know Her is to Know Him
Someone's Mistake
The Ginko Collector
Guns Aren't Destroying Our Country
The Concert
Standing United
Interpreters
They All Have Stories
A Writer

Laugh with Me

Laugh out loud with me
As I hide inside
No way out
Laugh with me

Within I am ripped
Alcohol and drugs cannot repair
Within darkness the deepening rip hides
Smiles hold back the pain
But don't erase it.

Laugh out loud with me
As I hide inside
No way out
Laugh with me

No light within the blackness
No hand can reach me
No comfort within the crowd
No joy within the laughs
Just me lost

Laugh out loud with me
As I hide inside
No way out
Laugh with me

I managed
I taught
I shared
I loved
I suffered

Laugh out loud with me
As I hide inside
No way out
Laugh with me

Behind you are left
Bewildered
Saddened
Educated

Laugh out loud with me
As I hide inside
No way out
Laugh with me

Reality has jolted
Understanding
Memories
Laughs

Laugh out loud with me
As I hide inside
No way out
Laugh with me

Now past laughs push towards change
Now past laughs remind of hidden pain
Now past laughs are insights to struggles

Laugh out loud with me
As I hide inside
No way out
Laugh for me

A Pen & Words

I want a pen
I need a pen
I need to murder the monster

Weapons won't due
There is too much power within
Its reign needs to end
Nothing has taken it out

I want a pen
I need a pen
I need to murder the monster

So many lives destroyed
So many deceived by words
So many left stripped of all
So many unwanted tears

I want a pen
I need a pen
I need to murder the monster

The pen will document its history
Faces with voices will be heard
Hands will join in force with words
Truth will be visible in ink

I want a pen
I need a pen
I need to murder the monster

Lives have been sliced apart
Yet determined they continue to stand
Now aware they are not alone
But an army of resilience

I want a pen
I need a pen
I need to murder the monster

Give me your words

Let them slice through the image projected
Reveal the monster's truth
Let it burn from the fire of truth

I want a pen
I need a pen
I need to murder the monster

An end has come
The façade ripped down
Even monsters can be revealed as weak
When voices find their words

I want a pen
I need a pen
I need to murder the monster

In Seconds We Drown

The aircraft carrier was sinking
Bombs ripped and burned its shell
Floating in an endless sea, you
Drowning in death
Drowning in survival

In seconds we drown
The jeans were ripped off
Body on top bruising and tearing flesh
Floating in endless loneliness, you
Drowning in shame
Drowning in survival

In seconds we drown
The bullet exploded from inside out
Blood burned as it splattered upon the skin
Floating in an endless nightmare, you
Drowning in loss
Drowning in survival

In seconds we drown
The silence screams within the walls
Emptiness smothered joy of living
Floating in endless depression, you
Drowning in sadness
Drowning in survival

In seconds we drown
The bottle swallows the body and memories
Recall haunting dreams with fear
Floating in endless terror, you
Drowning in self-hate
Drowning in survival

In seconds we drown

The fist impales the skin
Pain numbs against further strikes
Floating in endless suffering, you
Drowning in spilled blood
Drowning in survival

In seconds we drown
In seconds we can save

Protestor

You chant for the unborn,
But what about the born?
Those amidst the aftermath of birth,
Within the streets,
Within the shelters,
Within drug houses,
Within hospitals,
They survive.

You make time for the unborn,
But what about the born?
Those amidst the aftermath of birth,
Living life alone,
Within the streets,
Within the shelters,
Within drug houses,
Within hospitals,
They survive.

You spend hundreds on the unborn,
But what about the born?
Those amidst the aftermath of birth,
Living health-less, homeless, loveless,
Within the streets,
Within the shelters,
Within drug houses,
Within hospitals,
They survive,
And die.

Let Me

Let me push you
Not
Because you are helpless
But
Because I am thankful for my legs

Let me hold your hand
Not
Because you are helpless
But
Because I am thankful for my youth

Let me stand by your side
Not
Because you are helpless
But
Because I am thankful for my strength

Let me shout "STOP!"
Not
Because you are helpless
But
Because I am thankful for my voice

Let me welcome you
Not
Because you are helpless
But
Because I am thankful for I was never unwelcomed

Let me feel the fist
Not
Because you are helpless
But
Because I am thankful fist never broke my body

Let me hear the names
Not
Because you are helpless
But
Because I am thankful for not allowing them to define me

Let me help you up
Not
Because you are helpless
But
Because I am thankful for my ability to protect

I

I stopped breathing
Driving on through the memories
I held my breath in
I held my memories in

The past wrapped tentacles around
While I tried to enter without emotions
The past smells, sounds reached out
Crushing, forcing all to mash together

I stopped breathing
Driving on through the memories
I held my breath in
I held my memories in

Pictures smile with sarcasm
Trinkets replay movies of what was
A full closet contained the scent of us
Piles of notes capture our what ifs

I stopped breathing
Driving on through the memories
I held my breath in
I held my memories in

A discarded heap of before
Overwhelmed with loss
Squeezed by each tentacles of life
Air escaped while all else entered

I stopped breathing
Driving on through the memories
I held my breath in
I held my memories in

No longer, no more
But a future emerged ahead for one
Peeling back each tentacle
Paths without obstacles appeared

I stopped breathing
Driving on through the memories
I held my breath in
I held my memories in

Breathing begins again,
Just as I
As only I.

Enough

Enough blood to paint the land
Enough blood to color the seas
Has been spilled
And continues to spill

Tolerance enough to bar one door
Understanding enough to fill a book
Love enough to circle a state
Kindness enough to embrace a city

Enough blood to paint the land
Enough blood to color the seas
Has been spilled
And continues to spill

Enough hate to cover a world
Enough violence to touch everyone to our right and left
Enough sadness to shatter all hopes
Enough anger to break every spirit

Enough blood to paint the land
Enough blood to color the seas
Has been spilled
And continues to spill

Enough,
Yet not enough to bring ends.

Aging

Wish you understood my expression
As your hurtful words cut my heart,
But your mind is disappearing.

I see you,
But
You see the past,
You see an illusion.

I see you,
Explicit, violent words escape
the mouth which used to kissed good night.

I long to hear your love,
But your memory is decomposing.

From within you are a shell,
Outwardly you are my past,
My history,
My beginning,
My first love,
But now you are just a stranger.

A familiar face,
A familiar voice,
An unfamiliar embodied in the familiar,
As the past disappears,
As the love is crushed,
As the hatred replaces.

Gone, gone, gone
You.

Lost is what we are living
As age comes as Alzheimer's.

To Be Held

Religion
Meant to be held in your soul
God
Meant to be held in your thoughts
Spirituality
Meant to be held in your heart
Morality
Meant to be held in your actions
Kindness
Meant to be held in your words
Hope
Meant to be held in your out stretched hands
Humanity
Meant to be held in your arms

Espiritu Santo

In the quiet of a wind storm,

As the stars shot across the night sky,

Sleep came.

Under the golden, blazing sun,

On the rockery of Los Islotes,

Sitting still,

The beauty of nature and its animals emerged.

In the world under the sea's surface,

The sea lions flew,

As graceful as the frigates of the sky.

We came to discover the ecology of sea lions,

But discovered more.

Learning the ecology of man and nature,

While discovering life

And ourselves.

Walk with Me

Before you take that leap
Pull the trigger
Put that noose on
Take that pill
Down that last drink
Take a walk with me

Sit down and breathe
Look into the sky at sunset
Smile at a child
Before you make that final goodbye
I am life
One beginning
One end

Tomorrow can be different
Tomorrow can be better
Tomorrow should come
You matter
If to no one else
But me, life

So before
Take a moment with me
For there is no redo,
After is an end

A Walk Within the Forest

I went for a walk
Within the forest
To see who was hiding.
I found the lost dinosaurs
When his large feet slipped from behind the tree.
The giant sleepy turtle
Pushed out his head with closed eyes,
Then froze like stone.
Then within the midst of a yawn,
I saw a strange creature,
All snuggled down for its nap.
A shy crocodile hid under brush
Only its head visible.
Then the nosey dragon reared his head
Just to feel the sun rays.
Met up with the fairies
As they sunbathed upon a log.
Time was slipping by,
The old man of the trees,
Bid me goodbye.

Eve Is My Hero

She was a power house of inquiry
She challenged rules.
She chose answers over commands.
She found knowledge.

May every daughter grab the apple,
And not be content with following.
May every daughter seek answers to the unknown,
And not be content to ignore.
May every daughter find knowledge for change,
And not be content to remain still,

Eve is my hero,
Not to be condemned,
Not to be blamed,
Not to be less
For she was what was created.
A being of intelligence
Who sought knowledge through actions.

A creature with a mind of cravings,
A creature of beauty,
A creature of life,
Eve is my hero.
Not original sin
But original scientific method.
Eve was the first scientist
Not sinner.

Creators create,
But creations grow.
Bound by nothing,
Because they are new.
In the "image of" is not exact duplicate.
Eve was boundless.
Eve was Eve.

Eve is my hero.
May we all be Eve.
May we all be proud to be Eve.
Imagine where we'd be
If Eve were the celebrated hero.

Don't shoot

Riding my bike for the first time
Being held in grand-mom's embrace
Getting a cone from the ice cream truck
Playing tag on the hot asphalt
Just playing
Don't shoot

Sitting in my car seat
Speaking with family on the porch
Sleeping in my bed
Walking home from school
Just living
Don't shoot

Sitting in my stroller
Walking home from the store
Out with the dog for his last walk
Recounting our mother daughter night out
Just enjoying
Don't shoot

Working the register of the corner store
Checking in on the local businesses
Delivering a late-night meal
Answering the call for a ride
Just working
Don't shoot

Time

Time passes,

You grow.

The world changes,

You discover.

A friend dies

You mature.

Who Spilled the Glitter?

Who spilled the glitter?
Not me
Neither did I

A twinkling trail has been laid
I didn't do it
I didn't either

Upon the ground the glitter sparkles
I did it

A celestial body had become lost
And knew not the way to night

Taking your frosty glitter
I laid a twinkling trail
To reflect its light

When Moon's light winked back
Moon knew he'd found home
The darken sky above Earth

The Return

The scars inside
I cover with a uniform
The scars on the outside
I hide with a flag
The memories inside my mind
I drown with drinks
The nightmares behind close eyes
I crumple under within darkness

Upon a foreign land I buried my smile
Within foreign towns I scattered my innocence
In a foreign sea I drowned my happiness
Among the foreign population I slaughtered my heart
Engulfed by foreign rocket explosions I dropped my tears

I returned from foreign lands a shell
So many pieces gone
So much of me gone
So much not me

I went to the sea to seek my happiness from the crashing waves
I yelled to the smoke to return my tears
I returned map-less to the land to dig up my smile
I pleaded with all from abroad to return the pieces of my heart
I sought through the towns to locate my innocence

But it was too late
They were gone
I was barely a shell
I crumpled to the earth
Lost within the population
That did not, could not understand
I was lost

The scars inside
I cover with a uniform
The scars on the outside
I hide with a flag
The memories inside my mind
I drown with drinks
The nightmares behind close eyes
I crumple under within darkness

I failed

I tried to hold back the clouds
I tried to block the darkness
I tried to prevent the rain from falling
I tried to keep the chaos out
But I failed
Your tears flowed
Your anger burst
Your dark side engulfed
Your voices shouted

I tried to hold you together with hugs
I tried to soothe your voices with music
I tried to carry you to the light with only my strength
I tried to stop your tears with smiles
But I failed
You were missing
You were broken
You were hurt
You were scared

When the clouds scatter
When the rains end
When the darkness shatters with light
When the chaos dies
I will not fail
I will stand by you
I will find your voice
I will continue to love you
I will bring a hand to hold

Not alone
Not voiceless
Not isolated
Not forgotten
You and I as we

We will not fail
Because we understand
Because we refute statistics
Because we are stronger
Because we are survivors

Just another dinner

A small gesture
A meal
A bottle of wine
Two glasses

Time ticks by

One chair occupied
One glass filled
One meal eaten

Time ticks by

Another missed meal
Another together opportunity gone
Another night alone

Time ticks by

Lights off
Doors locked
Rooms emptied

Time ticks by

You arrived too late
As all are gone
But
Now you show up

Gone

When you became the wind,
Did you look back?
When you faded into the unknown,
Did you look back?
When the world turned black,
Did you look back?

When you disappeared,
I stood lost.

I looked back,
Asking what if?
As my heart shattered,
My soul crushed under pain.

I looked back,
Every day since,
But you were gone
And
I was as lost as you,
But
I looked back.

555 Lost

555 gone
The cure for cancer,
The engineering marvel,
Leader for justice,
Comic relief,
Solo artists,
Music prodigy,
Greatest mathematician,
Teachers,
Doctors,
And so much more
Lost.
Bullets ended futures,
Shattered lives,
Fragmented reality,
Exploded dreams,
Then splattered hurt,
Trauma,
Fear,
Onto ever wall of life.
Lives,
Beating hearts,
What could of
Is gone.
555 lives
555 futures
555 could have been
555 silent heartbeats
555 graves
555 lost
555 just children.
All in 3 years,
Our future
Short by 555*.

*Number of children under twelve who died between Dec. 14 2012 (Sandy Hook Elementary school shooting) and Dec. 14, 2015.

Lessons Learned

Years of repetition
Pamphlets reinforced
While speakers voiced the same

Don't walk alone
Don't be out late
Don't wear those

We are the reason
We are the perpetrators first
We are victims last

Don't walk alone
Don't be out late
Don't wear those

We are not free
We are not independent
We are not equal

Don't walk alone
Don't be out late
Don't wear those

We are a commodity
Picked up, tossed aside
Brutalized

Don't walk alone
Don't be out late
Don't wear those

The victims presented
The lessons' words echoed
In interviews, conversations, statements

Don't walk alone
Don't be out late
Don't wear those

We stand united under the wrong lessons
We are female
We deserve not to be raped

Don't rape

Don't attack

Don't blame

Men should walk in groups
Men should not be out late
Men should not hide behind hoodies
If men can't not rape

Don't rape

Don't attack

Don't blame

Penises should be properly covered
Owners should enroll in Don't Rape class
Requiring nightly escorted as they lack control

Update the lessons
Educate before discriminating
Justice not blame

Don't rape

Don't attack

Don't blame

Rape takes a victim
Society blames the victim
Education teaches avoidance

Don't rape

Don't attack

Don't blame

Stand in actions and words
Shout men will not rape
Demand men not rape

Don't rape

Don't attack

Don't blame

A $2 Dream

Bags at her feet
A knitted robe covers her
She feeds the dollars
To the lottery vending machine
Chooses her selections
Awaits her tickets
She looks over her selections
Checking their accuracy
Satisfied she gathers her bags
Departing on her trek home
Alone
Clutching her dreams
As the crumple within her hand.

Two Not Four

They walked with shoes untied
Shirts misbuttoned
As drop toys remain behind

There were only two hands
Not four

Two hands always filled
With life
With hands, bodies and more

There were only two hands
Not four

Two hands up-righted the fallen
Embraced the entire body
Hid the face for peek-a-boo smiles

There were only two hands
Not four

Strong enough to protect
Knowledgeable enough to guide
Powerful enough to teach

There were only two hands
Not four

Sometimes two is stronger than four
Sometimes two is more than enough
Sometimes two is all that is needed

There were only two hands
Not four

Two raised citizens of the world
Two pointed out the beauty of all
Two pushed to change the wrongs

There were only two hands
Not four

But were all we needed
Because they were mom's
Two hands

Reality

He's only six
Yet he wears a lifetime of suffering
Black eyes,
Bruised legs,
Bones protruding.
Quietly he chose the corner chair
Head down,
Legs dangling,
Lifeless,
Emotionless,
He's a body of pain,
From his interior depths,
To the exterior discolored skin.
Lost,
So long ago,
Was his child spirit.
Silenced,
So many beatings ago,
Were spontaneous laughs.
His childhood banished.
Now,
Just a body slumped
Upon a lone chair.

Deeds

He took their hands,
you took the bottle.
He pick them up,
you passed out on the floor.
He taught them to kick,
you taught them fear.
He showed them morals,
you showed them violence.
He patted them on the back,
you kicked them out of your house.
He showed them how to build,
you showed them how to destroy.
He show them respect,
you voiced you distaste.
He showed them love,
you only said you loved.
He provided what was needed,
you provided excuses.
His presence is always known,
your absence was never noted.

Today they shake a man's hand,
a man they proudly call dad,
by deeds not DNA.

Today

Guns held to heads,
Fires burn one home at a time,
Chalk body and bullet outlines multiple.

Fear, hate, violence,
All to bring control with power,
Conform or bleed.

Tears fall as quickly as fists,
Bruises discolor, while cuts bleed,
Silence engulfs cries for an end.

The metal of the weapons, grants courage.
The scars of the past, grant permission.
The entitlement mentality, grants amnesty.

Ends come with flash bangs,
Death was the finale,
Bleeding out was the pain bullying couldn't stop.

Life's Clutter

All the clutter of loneliness
     fills the home.
All the clutter of lost love
     piles upon every surface.
All the clutter of hate
     hides inside black garbage bags.
All the clutter of the past
     occupies the empty boxes stacked high.
All the clutter of sadness
     spills upon blackening floors.
All the clutter of happiness
     shouts from the greeting cards and gift wrap stacks.
All the clutter of age
     yellows with decay amongst the litter.
Clutter,
    Real
       or
       Emotional,
Piles up upon us
Hiding
    Truth,
        Pain,
           Fear,
              Lost.
Overwhelming,
Engulfing our true being.

Sailor Ashore

Broken
Lost
Sad

The ship now sails without you.
Upon the shores
You
Alone.

In battle you were fearless,
But
All was lost
All were lost.
You clung to the debris
Debris that was home,
Friends, life.
Within the cold arms of the sea
You clung
Not ready to die
But willing to
For country and family
You were a sailor
From your first days at 14,
It was in your heart
It was in your soul
You were released when the truth was discovered,
Only to return at 16.
The salt flowed from your sweat
As the sea pumped your heart
Your true loves were knotted
The sea and the sailor.
You left port with dreams,
Now you clung to the nightmare of reality
A sole survivor
Surrounded by death and destruction,
All being swallowed by the sea.
Would you be next?
Days would pass

As slowly as hope
In a daze you were rescued,
But were you?

They pinned the metals to your chest
As if they would mend the gashes from the losses
Your sea blue eyes were empty
Your soul was broken
Your love lost
Alone and broken upon the unforgiving shores
That neither bent nor wavered,
No matter how much you tried.

The ship sailed into the sea
Joining the lost comrades
Feeling their spirit
As well as lost.

You were broken
You were misunderstood
You found life within a bottle here
A bottle there
Anything to bring back the memories
Anything to erase the memories
You were a sailor
Now just broken
And lost
A sailor ashore.

Humanity

He ran into the building
She protected her brother from a kidnapper
He gave his dinner to the homeless
Someone saw their value
Understood they would be great
They were seen

He was two when he was sold
She was seven when she was given to a rapist
He was kidnapped at twelve
Nobody saw their worth
No one cared about their pain
They were never seen

He lost a limb
She died a hero
He will never be the same
They were rewarded
Humanity honoring humans

He was left in a pile of trash
She was discarded in the gutter
He was thrown from a cliff
Just trash
Still unseen

Humans without humanity's embrace.

Draped in the country's flag

Carefully
Six men,
Three on the right and left
Age has grayed, bent, and matured them,
But death broke their hearts.
Silently, in unisons
Hands glided across the brass bars
They slide their friend, brother, son
Onto its final viewing altar
Allowing it to come to rest
In full view of all.
Draped in his country's flag
A country he defended with a uniform
He wore it upon his chest
Gave his soul for it
Protected it with clenched fist
Wrapped its Stars and Stripes with mud covered arms
Raised it above foreign lands
Bled for it on burning battlefields
Embraced all its red, white, and blue symbolized
Saw the beauty of its captured stars
And those filling the sky above its land
Today, it wraps him in its stripes
Protecting him
Embracing him
Letting all know
His country did not forget.

Find yourself

Just find yourself
In a world so big,
Yet so small.

Don't get lost in words.
Don't get crushed by actions.
Don't get beaten by labels.

Just find yourself.

Before you become a label,
Find your heart.
Before you become a result,
Find your passion.
Before you give in,
Find you.

Just find yourself
To be yourself.

The Door Unlocked

I just wanted to leave the door unlocked
I just wanted to breathe
I just wanted to feel
I just wanted to let go

Doors shattered as much as hearts
Holes covered walls and us
Chaos covered the floor and our lives
No peace on the horizon
No reunion eminent

I just wanted to leave the door unlocked
I just wanted to breathe
I just wanted to feel
I just wanted to let go

Behind locks we hid
Behind closed windows we settled
Behind covered glass we told no secrets
Tension and anticipation wrapped us
There was no future you with us

I just wanted to leave the door unlocked
I just wanted to breathe
I just wanted to feel
I just wanted to let go

Each night the light went out
The manmade monster emerged
Waiting for the attack, after the hunt
It happened, it always did
As breath entered his body

I just wanted to leave the door unlocked
I just wanted to breathe
I just wanted to feel
I just wanted to let go

Breathing free, the monster hunted on
Chest tightened, fist clenched, breathing labored
No rest to come during the hunt
Just coward behind locked doors
While a plan was devised for attack

I just wanted to leave the door unlocked
I just wanted to breathe
I just wanted to feel
I just wanted to let go

Another statistic to be added
Another case closed while they were opened
Another bloody ending
Just bodies to be counted
For them, their war ended with a clear loser.

I just wanted to leave the door unlocked
I just wanted to breathe
I just wanted to feel
I just wanted to let go

The Past

Gouged holes
Hallowed out childhood memories,
Actions kept us from being children,
Pure, innocent, naïve.
Pain turned memories black
Then
We move on.

Educators

Stepping forward while looking back

To when you held our hands

While ascending the future

Memories created,

Friendships bonded,

Amongst the crowd maturity emerged

For brick walls held more than education

Life's trial began with first steps

Voices were found

Strengths were found

Paths were found

Awaited was potential

Stepping forward while looking back

To when you held our hands

While ascending the future

Work

Third playground within sight,
Sun shining and warming the air,
Ice cream truck music echoes down the street,
Behind glass windows they watch it all pass by.

Children play with caregivers looking on,
Green leaved trees sway in warm breezes,
Balls bounce into nets, through hoops, into gloves,
Enclosed in glass and metal they watch it all pass by.

Jackets discarded in piles against chain link fences
Games created, involving all who wish,
Joyous screams frequently yet spontaneously erupt,
Four wheels carry them away to streets lined only with houses.

No play today,
Work to be done,
Bills to be paid.

How

How do you believe?
How do you not?
How do you have such faith?
How do you not?
How do you keep it strong?
How did you let it get so weak?

Your world collided with reality,
You found faith.
My world collided with reality,
I found me, alone.

I led me,
Faith led you,
I held myself up with belief in self,
You stood tall with your faith as support.

How do you believe?
How do you not?
How do you have such faith?
How do you not?
How do you keep it strong?
How did you let it get so weak?

Hate, prejudice, and sadness were all about me,
I was lost amongst the negativity.
Love, support, and kindness mixed with the negativity,
But faith prevailed,
You were found and guided.
I stood strong,
Because I had no one to lean on.
You stood tall with faith by your side.

How do you believe?
How do you not?
How do you have such faith?
How do you not?
How do you keep it strong?
How did you let it get so weak?

Lost,
Found,
Happiness,
Happiness,
Amongst friends,
I found belief in humanity.
Amongst God,
You found belief in religion.

How do you believe?
How do you not?
How do you have such faith?
How do you not?
How do you keep it strong?
How did you let it get so weak?

Again

It's been too long
Since smiles came so quick,
Laughter spilled out.

At your touch,
Chills raced through my skin,
As a tickle escaped into each nerve.

Is it love?
As there is a longing for your touch,
Your energy.

Then you're gone
Again

Missing

The bed was occupied by emptiness,

I squeezed under the covers,

Only one breath echoed within the darkness,

Coldness swept across my skin,

Missing,

Blankets embraced,

Spontaneous conversations silent,

Darkness held tight,

Missing,

Missing you.

John Doe

Unknown,
A broken body,
Frozen in place,
Inside a heart use to beat,
Eyes use to focus on life,
Presence once made someone tingle within,
Where did he disappear to?
When did he become invisible.

Born Free, Die Free

Born free,
Die free,
Words to be read,
Words true for a few.

Born within boundaries,
Upholding personal freedoms,
Giving the perception of free,
But
Not for all,
Just some.

Born free is for the minority,
Of which I am not.

Born,
Died,
But not free,
Just female,
Able to read the words.

Sounds of summer

The sounds of summer are like gold.

Hoses dripping from the watering of the lawns,

The ringing bells of Mister Softee,

The rippling of the chlorine-treated pool water,

Summer games being played by the neighborhood kids,

Hide and Go Seek, Red Light, Green Light and Mother May I,

The tennis balls being smacked back and forth,

Motor scooters roaring,

Older boys playing football,

Radios blasting-

And then mothers calling kids in for dinner.

Teacher, My Teacher

Teacher, my teacher

You stood upon many a desk

Just to bring excitement

To the literature.

Teacher, my teacher

You shouted from many a window

So, we could feel the past

Within the lives of history.

Teacher, my teacher

You danced across many a stage

Hoping we'd feel the creativity

Captured within the works of artist.

Teacher, my teacher

You conversed in many a foreign cafe

Knowing we'd understand the beauty

Intertwined in languages of the world.

Teacher, my teacher

You unraveled many a puzzle

Understanding we'd unlock those mysteries

Cryptically written in math.

Teacher, my teacher

Your voice, mind and life now silent

Knowing we'd listen, recall and understand all you gave in time

Teaching the next generation to see all

Hidden within and outside education

Teacher, my teacher

May your lessons be forever.

To know her is to know him

He holds her hand gently,
Her braids bouncing.
He checks his pace to glide with her stride,
She smiles when she sees his eyes.
While carrying on an easy conversation,
He looks both ways before they cross.
He's not her father,
He's a better man than he.

He's a man,
Not in years but wisdom.
He's her brother,
Her teacher.

Teaching her what a man is,
He will protect her,
He will respect her,
Then he will demand that of every man
Who wishes to know her.
After all,
To know her,
Is to know the man who raised her.

Someone's Mistake

You may be someone's mistake
But not yours
You stand
With a past you never chose
With a future you choose

Words told the story
A mistake
Never wanted
Actions depicted the truth
A mistake
Never wanted

Left behind
Within the unknown
As chaos surrounded
Yet you rose upon your feet

Never seeing you as a mistake
You are strong
You are you
You are independent
You are beauty
You are not your mistake

Someone's DNA was a mistake
Someone's choices were a mistake
Someone's words were a mistake
Someone's actions were a mistake
But you,
You were not

Believing in you
Cheering on you
Being you
Living for you
Always choosing you
For you make choices
To exist

The Ginkgo Collector

Bent at the knees

Gathering the precious fruits

Fruits of her ancestors' land

Scattered about the urban landscape

Most lay rotting where they've fallen

There is no sweetness to ginkgo fruit rotting

Only decay and manure odors waft from them

But intertwined are the treasured

The pristine fruits worthy of being collected

Into the recycled grocery bag, they are dropped

Growing in numbers the bag begins to fill

After all are collected from one area the collector stands

Surveying the site one last time

She moves to the next tree and area

To start again

Hours in the coolness of the fall

She collects the precious fruit of her ancestors

Gathering this year's harvest

Once a year these precious fruits drop upon the city grounds

Their value stomped into the concrete by the naïve

But she knows their value

So, she collects.

Guns Aren't Destroying Our Country

Gun ownership
Isn't destroying our country.
Racism with guns,
Hate with guns,
Religion with guns,
Sexism with guns,
Alcohol with guns,
Stupidity with guns
Destroy lives,
End lives.
As bullets rip through skin,
Through organs,
Spilling out blood of country men,
Women,
Children.

No prayer within school walls
Doesn't destroy our country.
Entitlement,
Blame,
Intolerance,
Lack of respect,
Judgment,
Hate
Within school walls

Destroy lives,
End lives.
As words rip through skin,
Through hearts,
Spilling out tears of country men,
Women,
Children.

Courts without justice
Aren't destroying our country.
Silence within systems of justice,
Silence within the streets,
Silence within the chaos,
Silence within puddles of blood,
Silence within the prisons of fear
Destroy lives,
End lives.
As fear rips through skin,
Through our dreams,
Spilling out hope of country men,
Women,
Children.

The Concert

Piano chiming
Vocal cords vibrating words
All mingling for song

Words, music, voices
Evoking emotions with
In the heart, mind, soul

Moments, history
Revived inside hearts, minds
Time ticks, all has gone

Standing United

Why did it take rubber bullets?
Why did it take tear gas?
Why did it take water cannons in negative temperatures?
Why did it take blood?
Why did it take tears?
It is their land.
It is their lives.
It is their ancestral spirits.
It is their right.
Standing Rock,
United the Nations,
United hearts,
United voices
Standing as one.
One voice,
One fight,
One goal,
All standing
Upon one rock.
Earth
That of their ancestors,
Their nation,
Their lives,
Their future,
Their mother.
Mother Earth
Victory is today,
No matter how small,
A victory
For Earth,
For humans.

Interpreters

Words thousands of years old,
Bound together,
Meanings lost,
Language inverted,
Society changed.

Books
Words
Passed to generations to come
To interpret.

Books,
Words,
Dividing,
Segregating,
Instilling hate,
Breeding intolerance
Through misinterpretations.

Humans decades old,
Misunderstand,
Misinterpret,
Justify,
Isolate
Words thousands of years old.

Blood flows in rivers
For bound words.
Bodies strewn across earth's soil
For passages.
Hatred breeds inside hearts
For messages.
All thousands of years old.

Bound words,

Thousands of years old,
Raised above many human lives,
Caused for much violence.

Sacred words,
Sacred books,
Read by many,
Understood by few,
Followed by fewer,
Manipulate by thousands,
Distorted by many,
Just words,
Just human lives,
Lost upon lost.

They All Have Stories

In the streets invisible
On the steps invisible
Within a crowd invisible
Walking through the crowds invisible

They all have stories
Of love, loss, happiness, desperation
Of when they were someone
Stories of lives living

Under rags
Inside boxes
Within abandon buildings
Hiding from lost humanity

They all have stories
Of love, loss, happiness, desperation
Of when they were someone
Stories of lives living

A writer

Pictures built with words

Hugs, tears, laughter capture upon paper

Sharing struggles and euphoria with carefully chosen letter combinations

Forcing you to feel the pain of homelessness, PTSD, death
One syllable at a time

Sharing the joys of survival, birth, love
Word after word

Transporting you to new worlds, societies, cities
Paragraphs into paragraph

Pushing you away with truth, sadness, reality
Chapter upon chapter

A writer, I am

About the Author

After attending a new school each year from kindergarten to high school, J. Jones found her way to the Philadelphia High School for Girls then moved on to Cabrini University. After earning her BA in Education as well as her secondary education certification, she continued her education with master classes at Lincoln University, and writing classes with The Institute for Children's Literature, Institute for Writers, and Wesleyan University. Life then took over as she became a single mom of two and a business owner, her writing material began to grow and collected. A native Philadelphian, she relishes the city life, but she always loves the escapes to the beaches and mountains. Within the chaos of single mother-hood, she managed to show her children the city and world they are a small part of as well as their importance within it then sent them out to live and thrive in it. In 2017 she released her first poetry book, *A Glimpse of Today: Poetry Pictures*, and in 2018 she released a guide book for parents and caregivers of bullied students, *Taking Down a Bully: To Find Freedom*. Recently she earned her MA in English and Creative Writing from Southern New Hampshire University and is working full-time as a writer and educator.